ABC

Reptile Book

Jessica Lee Anderson

Paperback ISBN: 979-8-9899560-2-9

Many thanks to Clint Laidlaw (Clint's Reptiles) for reviewing this book for accuracy, and to Tabitha Blewett, Craig Randall, and Brian Parkhurst for the feedback.

In memory of Brian Barczyk, a reptile-loving legend. - JLA

Photo credits—Front Cover: Komodo-adv, Life On White, Shelly Still, Ralphs_Fotos (Tortoise), Life On White (Scaleless Corn Snake), Billion Photos (Green Iguana); Back Cover: Bob Eastman (Blue-Tongued Skink); Cover Page: Komodo-adv, Life On White, Shelly Still, burtonhill (Green Anole), Komodo-adv, (Panther Chameleon); Copyright Page: NaturesAuraPhoto (Eyelash Crested Gecko), Life On White (Freckled Monitor); Dedication Page: Anna Kucherova; p. 4: Life On White; p. 5: Craig Randall (RIP Captain Blackbeard); p. 6: rick734; p. 7: Brain E. Kushner; p. 8: Tempusfugit; p. 9: Farinosa; p. 10: Patrick Gijsbers; p. 11: lilithlita; p. 12: LagunaticPhoto; p. 13: Mark Kostich; p. 14: Libin Jose; p. 15: LeitnerR, olgysha2008; p. 16: tunatura; p. 17: Kaan Sezer; p. 18: Gabriel Ortiz; p. 19: Miropa, p. 20: Saúl Banda García Granados (IG: @untalsulban); p. 21: Anolis01; p. 22: Uckarintra; p. 23: John Audrey, NaturesAuraPhoto; p. 24: Life On White; p. 25: Andri_Priyadi, p. 26: Ken Griffiths, p. 27: Gerald Corsi; p. 28: David O'Brien; p. 29: kojihirano; p. 30: hnijar07, membio, Life on White, Uckarintra, slavadubrovin, MollyNZ (Tuatara); p. 30: Michael and Ava Anderson

This Book Belongs to:

_____

Varanus komodoensis

Bonus: the Komodo Dragon, or Komodo Monitor, is the heaviest of all lizards!

A is for Alligator

Alligator mississippiensis

Alligators are large reptiles with a huge tail that is strong enough to partially propel them out of the water. Their bite force is powerful enough to crush bones, and they swallow down chunks of food without chewing.

B is for Bearded Dragon

Pogona vitticeps

Bearded Dragons live in the wild in Australia, and given how good-natured they can be, they're kept as pets all over the world. They have a "beard" of spikes under their chins which is how they got their name.

C is for Chuckwalla

Sauromalus ater

Chuckwallas are a type of lizard that live in the desert. Chuckwallas don't drink water often because they get what they need from plants (and their bodies even have a special way of storing water).

D is for Diamondback Terrapin

Malaclemys terrapin

True to its name, the Diamondback Terrapin has diamond shaped rings on the top of its shell. The top part of a turtle's shell is called a carapace and the bottom part is called a plastron.

E is for Emerald Tree Boa

Corallus caninus

Emerald Tree Boas are a type of a non-venomous snake that live in trees (arboreal). The Emerald Tree Boa uses its tail and body to wrap around a branch where it will coil up and wait for a meal to come by.

F is for Fire Skink

Mochlus fernandi

The Fire Skink is brightly colored and has a snake-like appearance. In general, skinks have thicker necks, shorter legs, and longer bodies compared to other lizards.

G is for Galápagos Giant Tortoise

Chelonoidis niger

Galápagos Giant Tortoises are the world's largest tortoise and can live over 100 years! Unlike turtles, tortoises have feet like elephants, and they walk on their toes.

H is for Hawksbill Sea Turtle

Eretmochelys imbricata

Hawksbill Sea Turtles are known for their narrow head and a beak that is shaped like a hawk's beak. These sea turtles are endangered, meaning the species is in trouble and needs help to survive.

I is for Island Glass Lizard

Ophisaurus compressus

The Island Glass Lizard is long, slender, and has no legs! While it may look like a snake, legless lizards differ as they have moveable eyelids, ear openings, and their tongues have a different shape.

J is for Jackson's Chameleon

Trioceros jacksonii

Male Jackson's Chameleons have three horns while females don't (and females also tend to be lighter green or even red). Chameleons are different than other lizards because of their long, sticky tongues, the shape of their feet and body, and the way their eyes move.

13

K is for Knight Anole

Anolis equestris

The Knight Anole is also called the Cuban Giant Anole—it is one of the largest anole species. Anoles are similar to geckos though anoles have eyelids that move, plus they are awake more during the day.

L is for Leopard Gecko

Eublepharis macularius

Leopard Geckos have spots like a leopard which is how they got their name. Most geckos have special toe pads that allow them to grip to all kinds of surfaces, though Leopard Geckos are different—they don't have any!

M is for Mangrove Monitor

Varanus indicus

Mangrove Monitors spend much time in the water, sometimes even salty water! Monitors are a type of lizard with a thick body, powerful legs, and a long neck and tail.

N is for New Caledonian Giant Gecko

Rhacodactylus leachianus

The New Caledonian Giant Gecko is often called a Leachie because of its scientific name. They are the largest gecko species in the world!

O is for Olive Ridley Sea Turtle

Lepidochelys olivacea

Olive Ridley Sea Turtles get their name from the olive color of their heart-shaped shell. They spend most of their lives in the sea though females will come onshore to lay eggs in the sand.

P is for Plumed Basilisk

Basiliscus plumifrons

The Plumed Basilisk is a brightly colored lizard native to Central America. They have interesting feet and long toes that allow them to run on water!

Q is for Querétaran Dusky Rattlesnake

Crotalus aquilus

This venomous snake is native to Mexico and is also called the Querétaro Dusky Rattlesnake. Like other rattlesnakes, they are pit vipers—they have special heat-sensing pits that help them to find prey.

R is for Rhinoceros Iguana

Cyclura cornuta

Rhinoceros Iguanas are mostly herbivores—they eat things like fruit, berries, flowers, seeds, and leaves. Unlike other lizards, iguanas have small spikes along their bodies and a flap under their neck called a dewlap.

S is for Saltwater Crocodile

Crocodylus porosus

Saltwater Crocodiles (or "Salties" as they are called in Australia) are the world's largest living reptile! Their powerful jaws deliver one of the strongest bites in the world!

T is for Tokay Gecko

Gekko gecko

The Tokay Gecko is active at night (nocturnal) and arboreal, meaning it lives in the trees. Like most other geckos, the Tokay Gecko's eyelid (called a spectacle or brille) is fused shut, and they will lick their eyes to keep them moist and clean.

U is for Uromastyx

Uromastyx sp.

The Uromastyx is also called a Spiny-Tailed Lizard. They are vegetarians, meaning they eat plants, vegetables, and fruits.

V is for Veiled Chameleon

Chamaeleo calyptratus

Veiled Chameleons are arboreal—their grippy feet grab onto branches and their long tongues catch insects. Like many other chameleon species, they can change colors.

W is for Woma Python

Aspidites ramsayi

The Woma Python, also known as Ramsay's Python or the Sand Python, is a non-venomous snake native to Australia. They hunt at night, constricting (or squeezing) their prey before swallowing it whole—including venomous snakes!

X is for Xantus Leaf-toed Gecko

Phyllodactylus xanti

The Xantus Leaf-toed Gecko is sometimes simply called the Leaf-toed Gecko. Like some other lizards, this gecko can drop its tail to distract a predator.

Y is for Yellow-bellied Slider

Trachemys scripta scripta

Yellow-bellied Sliders are a type of turtle that call both the land and the water home. If there is a threat, they are like many other kinds of turtles—they will draw their heads and limbs into their shell for protection.

Z is for Zebra-tailed Lizard

Callisaurus draconoides

The Zebra-tailed Lizard lives in desert areas found in the southwestern part of the United States. Zebra-tailed Lizard hatchlings (babies recently hatched from eggs) can curl or wag their tails.

5 Reptile Facts

1 Reptiles are "cold-blooded"—they rely on the environment to control their body temperature.

2 Only non-avian reptiles are "cold-blooded"—biologist Clint Laidlaw prefers the term "poikilothermic." So, what are avian reptiles? BIRDS!

3 Reptile skin is covered in scales or bony plates—or both! Reptiles shed their skin or plates throughout their lives.

4 While many reptiles lay eggs, several snake and lizard species give live birth.

5 The main groups of reptiles include turtles, crocodilians (crocodiles/alligators/caiman/gharials/false gharials), lizards and snakes, plus the Tuatara which is in a group all on its own.

Jessica Lee Anderson is an award-winning author of over 50 books for young readers. She writes reptile-positive stories including the NAOMI NASH chapter book series. Jessica lives near Austin, Texas with her daughter, Ava, and husband, Michael. They have a pet corn snake named Ari they watched hatch from an egg. You can learn more about Jessica by visiting www.jessicaleeanderson.com.

Check out these other titles:

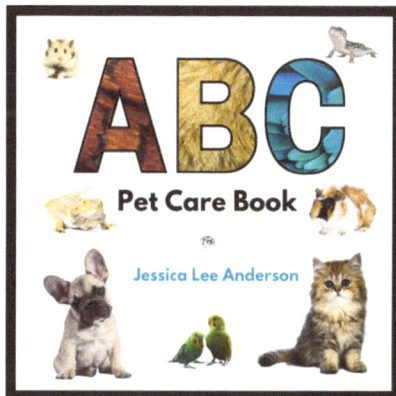

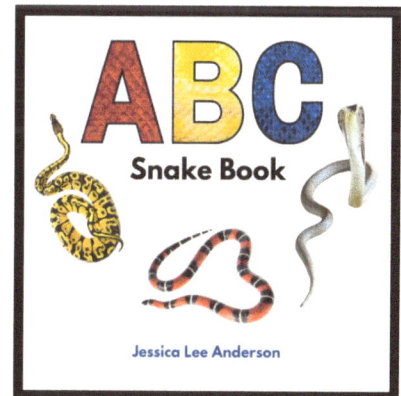

ABC Pet Care Book

Jessica Lee Anderson

ABC National Parks Book

Jessica Lee Anderson

ABC Snake Book

Jessica Lee Anderson

www.ingramcontent.com/pod-product-compliance
Lightning Source LLC
Chambersburg PA
CBHW061150030426
42335CB00003B/167